W9-BIH-938

KWJC

WOLVES

by Charnan Simon

Children's Press®

An Imprint of Scholastic Inc.
New York Toronto London Auckland Sydney
Mexico City New Delhi Hong Kong
Danbury, Connecticut

Content Consultant
Dr. Stephen S. Ditchkoff
Professor of Wildlife Sciences
Auburn University
Auburn, Alabama

Photographs © 2012: age fotostock: 31 (Michael Weber), 16
(Thomas Kitchin & Vict); AP Images: 36 (Phil Coale), 35 (Sergei
Grits); Bob Italiano: 44 foreground, 45 foreground; Dreamstime:
cover (Evan66), 44 background, 45 background (Sergey Revich),
2 background, 3 background (Socrates); Minden Pictures/Yva
Momatiuk & John Eastcott: 35, National Geographic Image
Collection/Paul Nicklen: 12; National Park Service/Yellowstone
National Park: 19, 24; Photo Researchers: 11, 23 (Jeff Lepore), 27
(Mark Hallett Paleoart), 40 (Tom McHugh); Shutterstock, Inc.: 1,
2 inset, 32 (Helen E. Grose), 8 (Matthew Jacques); Superstock: 5
bottom, 15 (age fotostock), 28 (Animals Animals), 4, 5 background, 7
(Flirt), 39 (Minden Pictures), 5 top, 20 (Science Faction).

Library of Congress Cataloging-in-Publication Data
Simon, Charnan.
   Wolves/by Charnan Simon.
      p. cm.—(Nature's children)
   Includes bibliographical references and index.
   ISBN-13: 978-0-531-20909-7 (lib. bdg.)
      ISBN-10: 0-531-20909-1 (lib. bdg.)
   ISBN-13: 978-0-531-21084-0 (pbk.)
      ISBN-10: 0-531-21084-7 (pbk.)
   1. Wolves—Juvenile literature. I. Title. II. Series.
   QL737.C22S55 2012
   599.773—dc23   2011031702

1 2 3 4 5 6 7 8 9 10 R 21 20 19 18 17 16 15 14 13 12

Wolves

Class	Mammalia
Order	Carnivora
Family	Canidae
Genus	*Canis*
Species	*Canis lupus* (gray wolf); *Canis rufus* (red wolf); *Canis simensis* (Abyssinian wolf)
World distribution	Mainly live in Russia, Alaska, and Canada; smaller numbers live in the northern United States, Asia, India, and the Middle East
Habitats	Can survive in a wide variety of environments, including woodlands, forests, prairies, grasslands, deserts, and tundra; most wolves today live mainly in remote wilderness areas
Distinctive physical characteristics	Most wolves have a gray and brown fur coat, with lighter colored fur on their faces, legs, and bellies; some are solid black or white; most are about 26 to 32 inches (66 to 81 centimeters) tall at the shoulder; females weigh about 80 pounds (36 kilograms); males weigh about 90 pounds (41 kg)
Habits	Highly intelligent and social; live together in family groups known as packs; hunt cooperatively to capture prey
Diet	Large hoofed mammals such as deer, elk, bison, caribou, and moose; smaller mammals such as beavers, rabbits, and mice

Contents

CHAPTER 1

Meet the Wolf

Wolves are members of the **canine** family. They look a little like German shepherd dogs. They have strong, muscular bodies and long, bushy tails. Most wolves have grayish-brown fur and lighter markings on their faces, legs, and bellies. Some wolves are solid black or white.

Wolves are among the most social animals on Earth. They live in family groups called **packs**. Pack members work together to help care for **pups**. Wolves are playful and loyal to their fellow pack members.

Wolves are also fierce hunters. They'll eat almost anything they can catch and kill. They mostly prefer to eat animals such as deer, moose, caribou, and elk. It takes strength and skill to kill such large animals. Wolf packs work together to bring down their **prey**.

Most scientists think that wolves are the **ancestors** of today's pet dogs. Even today, wolves and dogs share some common characteristics.

Wolves form close bonds with their fellow pack members.

8

Disappearing from the World

Wolves can survive in almost any **habitat**. They are able to live in both the frozen Arctic **tundra** and hot deserts. Wolves do not have many enemies among other wild animals. Even bears and lions avoid attacking wolf packs.

Wolves could once be found throughout most of the world. But people have hunted, trapped, and poisoned vast numbers of wolves over the years. As a result, wolves have disappeared from many of the places they used to live. They now live mostly in remote wilderness areas that are far away from people.

Wolves are **endangered** in some areas of the world. Some people are working to increase wolf populations. But scientists still fear that some types of wolves may become **extinct** if people don't do more to protect them.

Wolves that live in colder habitats often have lighter fur to help them blend in with the snow.

CHAPTER 2

Born to Hunt

Wolves are **carnivores**. This means they must hunt and kill other animals. Wolves sometimes eat small animals such as rabbits and mice. But they prefer large hoofed animals.

Wolves are built for strength and **endurance**. They can run for hours at a time and reach speeds of up to 40 miles per hour (64 kph) in short bursts. This helps them catch up to fleeing prey.

Most wolves are about 40 to 60 inches (102 to 152 cm) long. They can weigh anywhere from 40 to 175 pounds (18 to 79 kg).

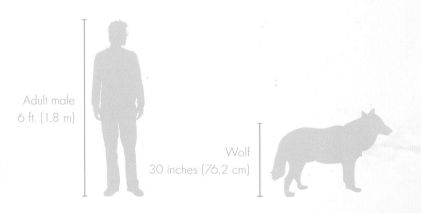

Adult male
6 ft. (1.8 m)

Wolf
30 inches (76.2 cm)

Large paws act like snowshoes to keep wolves from sinking into deep snow.

Eyes, Nose, and Ears

Wolves rely on their senses to help them hunt and survive. Their sharp eyes notice even very small movements. Wolves are especially good at seeing in the dark. They can spot prey or threats from more than 1 mile (1.6 km) away.

Wolves have large ears that allow them to hear very well. They are always listening for danger. Their sharp hearing also lets them communicate with pack members over great distances. Wolves can hear their pack members howling from as far away as 10 miles (16 km).

Wolves have a very strong sense of smell. They use their noses to find prey and avoid danger. A wolf's sense of smell is almost 100 times better than that of a person. Wolves have been known to pick up the scent of a moose from a distance of 1.5 miles (2.4 km).

Wolves can see at night much better than humans can.

Strong and Sharp

Wolves use their strong jaws and sharp teeth to kill and eat their prey. A wolf's jaw is twice as powerful as a large dog's. Wolves need strong jaws to hunt and kill the large, fast animals that they like to eat.

A wolf has 42 teeth. People have only 32 teeth. A wolf has four long, sharp canine teeth in the front of its mouth. These fangs can be 2.5 inches (6.4 centimeters) long. Wolves use their fangs to grab and kill prey. They use other, smaller, sharp teeth to tear away skin and cut through muscle. A wolf's strong back teeth are powerful enough to crush thick bones.

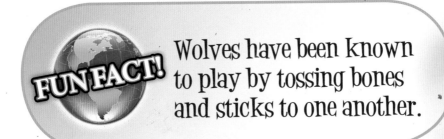

FUN FACT! Wolves have been known to play by tossing bones and sticks to one another.

Wolves show off their teeth to threaten other wolves.

Feast or Famine

An adult wolf needs to eat around 7 pounds (3 kilograms) of meat each day to stay healthy. They can survive on less if they need to, though. Wolves have large stomachs. A very hungry wolf can eat as much as 20 pounds (9 kg) of food at a time.

Wolf packs spend most of their time hunting. They track down and chase many more animals than they actually catch. The wolves may back off if a moose or elk fights back too strongly. The pack may also give up if the prey runs away too quickly. Wolves often chase ten or twelve animals before catching just one.

When hunting is poor, wolves sometimes go for a week or longer without eating. They can't afford to be picky once they finally make a kill. The wolves eat as much of the dead prey as they can.

A pack of wolves can quickly finish eating a large animal such as a deer.

CHAPTER 3

Life in a Wolf Pack

Wolves are very social animals. They live in family groups called packs. A typical wolf pack has six to eight family members. Some packs may have as many as 20 wolves.

Each wolf pack lives and hunts in a specific area called a **territory**. A pack's territory might be only 30 square miles (78 square kilometers) if there is plenty of food around. But sometimes wolves must roam much farther to find food. They might hunt animals such as caribou, which travel over huge areas. Some wolf packs cover a territory of more than 1,000 square miles (2,600 sq km). Wolves do not let wolves from other packs hunt in their territory. They attack and kill these rival wolves.

Adult wolves are strong and fierce. They do not have any natural **predators**. A wolf can live up to 13 years in the wild if it gets enough food and doesn't get injured.

Wolves are among the strongest hunters in their habitats.

Leaders of the Pack

The most powerful member of a wolf pack is called the **alpha** male. He leads the pack with the help of the strongest, healthiest female. She is called the alpha female. The alpha male and female are the **dominant** wolves in the pack. All of the other pack members must show respect for their leaders.

The alpha male and female generally mate for life. They are often the only wolves in the pack that have pups. This is because they work to prevent the other wolves in the pack from mating.

Each spring, the alpha female digs out a safe **den** and gives birth to a litter of four to six pups. At first the pups just sleep and drink their mother's milk. They begin to take their first wobbly steps outside the den after about three weeks. The pups practice skills they'll need as adults as they wrestle and play together.

The alpha male and alpha female share a close bond.

Helping Pups Grow Up

All the wolves in the pack help to care for the pups. One adult stays behind as a babysitter whenever the rest of the pack goes hunting. This babysitter protects the pups from predators such as bears and cougars.

The adults feed the pups by coughing up food they have already chewed and swallowed. Puppy teeth aren't strong enough to chew raw meat on their own. The adult wolves also take turns playing with the pups.

The pups leave the den when they are about two months old. The adults move them to a series of places called **rendezvous sites**. The pups play and sleep here while the adults hunt and bring back food.

By winter, the pups are old enough to join the hunt. Some pups stay with the same pack for their entire lives. Others move away to form their own packs when they are two or three years old.

Wolf pups form close bonds with their older relatives.

Hunting in a Pack

Raising pups is not the only job that wolf packs do together. They also work together to hunt. Wolves eat large animals like moose and elk. A moose might weigh 10 times as much as an adult wolf. A single wolf could never kill such a large animal by itself.

The alpha male decides when and where to hunt. He guides the pack in covering an area and searching for food. Wolves howl to alert the rest of the pack when they see or smell prey. The wolves then gather together and go in for the kill. Hunting large **mammals** with hooves and horns can be dangerous for the wolves. They must be careful not to get kicked or stepped on.

The alpha male and female are always the first to eat. Other animals such as bears sometimes try to steal the wolves' food. Hunting in a pack allows the wolves to take turns eating and chasing away other animals.

Wolves surround their prey to prevent it from escaping.

Out of the Past

Wolves have lived on Earth for a very long time. Scientists believe that the very earliest wolf ancestors first appeared around 60 million years ago. These ancestors did not look much like wolves do today. They were related to the ancestors of today's cats and foxes. Some of the earliest wolf ancestors could even climb trees.

Over millions of years, those ancient animals grew and changed. The first modern gray wolf probably appeared about a million years ago. Scientists believe that gray wolves may have first lived in Europe and Asia. They think wolves traveled to North America around 750,000 years ago.

Today's wolves are not related to cats and foxes. Instead, they belong to the *Canis* genus. *Canis* is the Latin word for "dog." Wolves, coyotes, jackals, and pet dogs are all in the *Canis* genus.

Large wolf ancestors called dire wolves once lived in North America.

Different Species

Scientists today argue about how many different **species** of wolves there are. They all agree on two species: the gray wolf (*Canis lupus*) and the red wolf (*Canis rufus*). Some scientists argue that there is also a third species called the Abyssinian wolf. Other scientists believe that the Abyssinian wolf is more like a jackal than a wolf. Abyssinian wolves are found only in certain parts of Ethiopia. They are smaller than gray wolves.

Gray wolves are the most common wolves. They are also known as timber wolves. There are many **subspecies** of gray wolves. They all share many of the same traits. They are intelligent and social, they live in family groups called packs, and they are expert hunters.

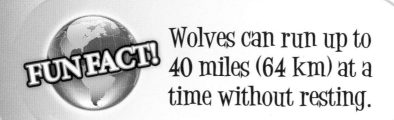

FUN FACT! Wolves can run up to 40 miles (64 km) at a time without resting.

Abyssinian wolves' red coloring and small size make them easy to tell apart from other wolf species.

Of Wolves and Dogs

Most scientists think that **domestic** dogs originally came from wolves. People began making friends with certain types of wolves at least 12,000 years ago. These early dogs may have been guard dogs. They may have helped people hunt. In exchange, people fed the dogs and gave them shelter.

No one knows exactly how or when wild wolf ancestors were domesticated. But over many thousands of years, dogs gradually became "man's best friend."

Most modern dogs don't look much like wolves. But dogs and wolves are alike in many ways. They are intelligent and loyal. They have sharp eyes, ears, and noses. They show affection by wagging their tails and licking each other's muzzles. They bow down and slap the ground with their front legs when they feel playful. They communicate by growling, whining, and barking.

Dogs are different from wolves in one important way. Even the fiercest guard dog is tame. But wolves are wild.

Wolves play and wrestle with each other just as domestic dogs do.

CHAPTER 5

What Does the Future Hold?

Wolves can survive in more habitats than any other land mammal except humans. They lived all over the world for thousands of years.

But throughout history, wolves have often had a bad reputation among humans. Many people hated wolves. They were afraid of the wolves' sharp teeth and spine-tingling howls. They told stories about wolves eating people, even though wolves almost never attack humans. Many believed that the only good wolf was a dead wolf.

Not everyone hated wolves. Many Native American tribes considered wolves to be **sacred** animals. They admired the wolf's hunting skills and loyalty to its pack members. They respected the wolf's strength and intelligence. They told stories in which wolves were heroes instead of villains. Native Americans and wolves lived peacefully with one another for centuries.

Wolves often howl after becoming separated from their packs.

The War Against Wolves

European settlers in the United States felt differently. Farmers didn't like wolves because they killed cows and sheep. Wolves killed even more cows and sheep after settlers killed many of the bison that wolves had previously hunted. Settlers also wanted to build new towns and farms on the wolves' land. Less wilderness land meant less room for wolves.

Wolves once ranged all across North America. Today, wolves have disappeared from almost all of the places where they used to live in the United States. Hunters killed thousands of wolves. Trappers killed thousands more.

Even the U.S. government got involved. For more than 100 years, the government offered a **bounty** to anyone who killed a wolf. Some individual states paid these bounties until the 1960s. Government programs also used poison to kill wolf packs around the country. The same thing happened in Europe and Asia.

By the early 1970s, there were only a few hundred wolves left in the United States outside of Alaska.

Wolves in Alaska hunt prey in large packs.

The U.S. Government Helps Out

People in the United States eventually realized that something had to be done. Wolves were in danger of becoming extinct. When an animal is extinct, it is gone forever. There's no bringing it back.

Once again, the U.S. government got involved. But the government was on the wolves' side this time. Gray and red wolves were among the first animals protected by the Endangered Species Act of 1973. This meant that wolves could no longer be hunted, trapped, or poisoned outside of Alaska. It also meant that the government would try to bring wolves back to wild areas of the United States.

Gray wolves have since made a comeback in several parts of the United States. There are about 3,000 wolves in northern Minnesota. Michigan and Wisconsin each have more than 500 wolves. At least 7,000 wolves roam throughout Alaska.

Scientists captured wolves and spread them into habitats where they were close to disappearing.

Wolves in Yellowstone

In 1995, 14 wild gray wolves from Canada were set free in Yellowstone National Park in Wyoming. It was the first time wolves had roamed Yellowstone in 70 years. Seventeen more wolves were released in 1996. The wolves quickly formed packs. They had pups, and those pups grew up and formed more packs. Today, there are about 1,500 wolves living in and around Yellowstone.

Many people didn't like the idea of releasing wolves into Yellowstone. Nearby ranchers worried that wolves would attack their livestock. Hunters thought that wolves might kill off too many elk and deer.

A fund was set up to pay ranchers for any livestock that was killed by wolves. People soon discovered that wolves would not destroy the deer and elk herds. Wolf packs tend to hunt animals that are sick, old, or inexperienced. Wolves may actually help keep elk and deer herds healthy by weeding out the weakest animals. They keep nature in balance.

Wolf populations continue to grow in Yellowstone National Park.

Helping Wolves Today

Red wolves have had a harder time staying alive. There were very few red wolves left in the United States by the 1960s. Scientists captured 17 of them to help save the species. They bred the wolves in zoos and carefully rereleased them into the wild. Today, there are more than 100 wild red wolves living in North Carolina. Another 200 live in zoos across the country.

Wolves still need our help. There are about 200,000 wolves living in 57 countries around the world. But some gray wolf subspecies, such as the Indian wolf and the Mexican wolf, are still in danger of becoming extinct. Hunters in Alaska use airplanes to legally chase and shoot wolves. Some people want to make it legal to hunt wolves again in the rest of the United States.

Humans played a major role in killing wolves around the globe. It is up to us to play a different role now. Only we can restore wolves to their rightful place in our shared world.

Today, most red wolves live in zoos.

Words to Know

alpha (AL-fuh) — the most highly ranked member of a group

ancestors (AN-ses-turz) — ancient animal species that are related to modern species

bounty (BOUN-tee) — a reward offered for the capture of an animal that is thought to be harmful

canine (KAY-nine) — of or having to do with dogs

carnivores (KAR-nih-vorz) — animals that eat meat

den (DEN) — the home of a wild animal

domestic (duh-MES-tik) — tamed

dominant (DAH-muh-nint) — most influential or powerful

endangered (en-DAYN-jurd) — at risk of becoming extinct, usually because of human activity

endurance (en-DOOR-uhns) — the ability to do something difficult for a long time

extinct (ik-STINGKT) — no longer found alive

genus (JEE-nuhs) — a group of related plants or animals that is larger than a species but smaller than a family

habitat (HAB-uh-tat) — the place where an animal or a plant is usually found

mammals (MAM-uhlz) — warm-blooded animals that have hair or fur and usually give birth to live young

packs (PAKS) — groups of wolves

predators (PREH-duh-turz) — animals that live by hunting other animals for food

prey (PRAY) — an animal that's hunted by another animal for food

pups (PUHPS) — baby wolves

rendezvous sites (RAHN-day-voo SITES) — places where wolves leave their young while going off to hunt

sacred (SAY-krid) — very important and deserving great respect

species (SPEE-sheez) — one of the groups into which animals and plants of the same genus are divided

subspecies (SUHB-spee-sheez) — groups of animals that are part of the same species, but share important differences

territory (TER-i-tor-ee) — area of land claimed by an animal

tundra (TUHN-druh) — a very cold area of northern Europe, Asia, and Canada where there are no trees and the soil under the surface of the ground is always frozen

NORTH

AMERICA

PACIFIC

ATLANTIC

OCEAN

SOUTH
AMERICA

Wolf Range

ARCTIC OCEAN

EUROPE

ASIA

AFRICA

PACIFIC
OCEAN

OCEAN

INDIAN

OCEAN

AUSTRALIA

Find Out More

Books

Goldish, Meish. *Red Wolves: And Then There Were (Almost) None*. New York: Bearport Publishing, 2009.

Markle, Sandra. *Family Pack*. Watertown, MA: Charlesbridge, 2011.

Read, Tracy C. *Exploring the World of Wolves*. Richmond Hill, ON: Firefly Books, 2010.

Web Sites

International Wolf Center—Wild Kids
www.wolf.org/wolves/learn/justkids/kids.asp
Enjoy fun activities and learn more about the lives of wolves.

National Geographic Kids—Gray Wolves
http://kids.nationalgeographic.com/kids/animals/creaturefeature/graywolf/
Learn cool facts, watch a video of a wolf pack at play, listen to the haunting sound of a wolf pack howling, and more.

Wolf Education Research Center—Wolf Behavior 101
www.wolfcenter.org/wolf-behavior.aspx
Learn more about how wolves move and communicate with each other.

Visit this Scholastic web site for more information on wolves:
www.factsfornow.scholastic.com

Index

(Index continued)

About the Author

Charnan Simon is a former editor of *Cricket* magazine and has written more than 100 books for young readers. She hopes someday to hear a wolf pack howling in the wild.